Ashley Warner

The Year After
Journal

*Your Guide to
Reclaiming Personal Power
After Rape*

PYTHIAN PRESS
NEW YORK

Copyright © 2016 Ashley Warner

All rights reserved.

ISBN: 0692790454
ISBN-13: 978-0692790458

This journal is dedicated to YOU.

ESSAYS

	Acknowledgements	1
1	How to Use This Journal	3
2	Presence in Pain	34
3	But What Do I Do About It?	68
4	Creative Healing	106
5	Sex	138
6	Fight, Flight, *Freeze*	178
7	Memory and Rape	212
8	Creative Healing—Dance and Music	246
9	It's Not Easy to Report Rape. Here's Why.	274
10	How to Help Someone Who's Been Sexually Assaulted Without Making Things Worse	314
11	Summing Up/ Looking Ahead	353
	Creative Healing—Activities	355
	Resources	359

ACKNOWLEDGMENTS

With thanks to some special people who lent extra support to this project: Blethyn Hulton, for editing prowess and infectious enthusiasm; Whitney Hamilton and Patrick Sullivan, for creative contributions and general awesomeness; James Giacinto, for lots of belly laughs and endless generosity as my partner in development; and Hugo Fernandez, whose love sustains me.

1

HOW TO USE THIS JOURNAL

When I was recovering from rape, I continued to keep a journal, just as I had done for many years (and still do!). I didn't write in it every day. Most days. Sometimes, all I could manage was a scribbled word or phrase about how I felt. "Lonely," "cautiously optimist," and "I want to rip someone's eyeballs out" are just a few examples of the rollercoaster of emotion found on the pages of my notebooks. One day's entry was nothing more than violent scratch made while holding a pencil in my fist like a small child. No words would suffice that day.

Decades later, the same journal entries grew into *The Year After: A Memoir*. In the aftermath of my assault, I had always wondered about the day-to-day experience of other victims of sexual violence. Did other people feel as crazy as I did? Did it seem just as hopeless? Although I found some excellent books and articles, none offered the unapologetic, from-the-trenches perspective I craved. So I wrote the book I had wanted to read but didn't exist. I'm proud that many of you have found *The Year After* helpful and inspiring.

This is your *Year After*. Whether you are a recent survivor or revisiting your trauma after many years, this guide is set up to help you. It is my heartfelt intention that on these pages you will find comfort. Even more, I hope you will find your way to deeper personal understanding, greater compassion for self and others, enhanced relationships, and improved ability to create the good life you are meant to lead. You deserve it!

Here's how the journal is laid out: it's like a weekly planner without days or dates—you provide those. The "calendar" is a year long. Of course, you can choose to write as many entries as you like each day; you don't need to follow a schedule. You can always continue with a second journal or repeat the course in another notebook.

Each entry also asks you to jot down how you feel. Answer quickly, without thinking too much. How do you feel right *now*? Not five minutes ago—*now*. If you don't know, or if you feel numb, that's your answer. It will be interesting to observe how your awareness shifts throughout the journaling process.

Next, a short writing prompt is provided to inspire your associations. Don't think too much about your responses here, either. To get the full benefit of the exercise, write what pops into your mind first. Reflect on it later. The prompts are purposefully vague, with no right or wrong interpretation. Use them to access what occurs to *you*. If you hate the prompt, write about why or skip it. This is your journey. You must always begin with your truth, or else any so-called progress will feel empty.

Inevitably, the prompts, or life at large, will inspire further exploration. If you're holding this book in paperback, which I recommend, plenty of blank pages follow on which to write. There is something most intimate and soothing about a pen gliding across the pages in your own hand. The book becomes a part of you, born from you. It is your work of art. You can doodle in the corners, use color, glue glitter. It might turn into something you keep forever.

If you're reading on an electronic device, or journaling on a computer, I hope you'll take the time to complete some of the exercises the old-fashioned way. Do you note any difference?

In addition to prompts and blank pages for free-style journaling, this book includes short essays on topics of healing that draw from my personal life as well as my experience as a psychotherapist. There's information about the healing power of creative arts, which I hope you'll find as interesting and useful as I do. Try some of the creative healing activities on page 355, which are in no particular order, whenever you wish. If you feel like it, visit me on Facebook and post some of your creations. *Only* if it feels right to share.

I'm ever grateful that my own story has a happy ending. But I won't lie: I found the road to recovery after rape to be arduous and messy. Worth it! Yet painful. Writing it all down helped me create structure again out of rubble. Of course, your journey will be unique. I've listened many, many stories of recovery and every one is different. Some people struggle mightily, others wonder why they don't feel worse, and almost everyone worries they aren't doing it "right." No matter what you encounter along your path, may you find a patient and comforting companion in these pages. I also hope you won't hesitate to reach out for help when necessary.

Although a journal is a wonderful tool (one of my favorites!), it's not everything. As for me, I found both individual and group psychotherapy to be instrumental to my healing. Sexual assault can be an isolating experience, and it's easy to give up on others. Sometimes we want to curl into a ball and keep the world away. Yet we've got to have people on our team, too. We shouldn't go mountain climbing alone, either.

With that, I turn it over to you. An adventure awaits.

For help locating your nearest counseling center, the Rape, Abuse, and Incest National Network website is a wealth of information and resources at RAINN.org. If you need to speak to someone immediately, the National Sexual Assault Hotline, 1-800-656-HOPE, operates 24/7 and is completely anonymous and confidential unless the caller chooses otherwise.

Date and time:

I feel:

I hope:

Date and time:

I feel:

It's hardest when:

Date and time:

I feel:

When I think of myself a year from now:

Date and time:

I feel:

I haven't told anyone that:

Date and time:

I feel:

Sometimes it seems:

Date and time:

I feel:

I can't stop thinking about:

Date and time:

I feel:

When I'm working:

What lies behind us and what lies before us are tiny matters compared to what lies within us.

Ralph Waldo Emerson

Date and time:

I feel:

I barely let myself:

Date and time:

I feel:

Sometimes I don't want to feel better:

Date and time:

I feel:

When I think of the unknown:

Date and time:

I feel:

If I could be anywhere:

Date and time:

I feel:

If I had it to do over again:

Date and time:

I feel:

When I'm angry:

Date and time:

I feel:

If I could say anything to anybody:

> *I celebrate myself, and sing myself.*
> Walt Whitman

Date and time:

I feel:

I know I feel because:

Date and time:

I feel:

When I close my eyes:

Date and time:

I feel:

My body:

Date and time:

I feel:

Nobody ever told me:

Date and time:

I feel:

Death:

Date and time:

I feel:

Three things I love:

Date and time:

I feel:

When I was five:

The wound is the place where the Light enters you.

Rumi

Date and time:

I feel:

I'm grateful for:

Date and time:

I feel:

Something I've always wanted to do:

Date and time:

I feel:

Something no one knows about me:

Date and time:

I feel:

I feel safest when:

Date and time:

I feel:

Now's a good time to:

Date and time:

I feel:

My favorite place:

Date and time:

I feel:

Something I'm really proud of:

We must be patient with the healing process.
The psyche knows what it can handle—listen to it.

The Year After

Date and time:

I feel:

I never thought:

Date and time:

I feel:

If I didn't know me:

Date and time:

I feel:

I really feel:

Date and time:

I feel:

When I start to feel overwhelmed:

Date and time:

I feel:

I'm scared that:

Date and time:

I feel:

One good thing that happened recently:

Date and time:

I feel:

My sense of humor:

Start by doing what's necessary; then do what's possible; and suddenly you are doing the impossible.

Francis of Assisi

2

PRESENCE IN PAIN

One sunny spring afternoon when I was 24 years old and a relatively new transplant to New York City, a stranger who had been hiding in my apartment building followed me up the stairs, grabbed me by the neck as I opened my door, and raped me at knifepoint. Shortly thereafter, I recalled with scorn a piece of advice my grandpa had lovingly imparted when I thought I already knew everything. On the eve of my move to the Big Apple to start my life as a full-fledged adult, he had taken me aside for a chat in my mother's kitchen. "Life is about the journey," he had counseled, "not the destination." Me: eyeroll. "Embrace your challenges and look for the blessings of each day."

"Got it," I had thought. Then I was raped.

Sometimes, our troubles are an inconvenience—something that didn't go as planned. Other times, problems are unjust and brutal, forced upon us by violence, abuse, or discrimination. How do we embrace the moment when to stand still is torture? How do we find blessings in days that have brought senseless harm, grief, or suffering? Better yet, why should we?

In the aftermath of big trauma such as rape, it's often impossible to be emotionally present. That's normal. It's expectable to experience weeks or even months of numbness or disconnection as the psyche tries to make sense of what doesn't make sense. It's also common to feel detached or out of sorts at tough points during the healing process.

Sometimes the way the wind blows is enough to shut us down- even after we've been feeling great again.

When floods of memories and feelings do emerge, the intensity might seem too overwhelming to tolerate, especially in the beginning. As for me, I slept with the television on for almost a year, took fast, angry walks, and screamed into pillows regularly. I ate an extraordinary amount of hamburgers—they're all I seemed to want. There is nothing wrong with seeking whatever small comfort can be found, and I encourage you to be generous with yourself!

When the intense distress finally dies down, it's tempting to say "later" to feelings altogether. Pushing emotions away might seem for a time like getting rid of them. Yet like a Whac-A-Mole at the county fair, those buggers are going to keep popping up. What's more, trying to do away with unpleasant emotions makes things worse. In fact, research has shown that trying not to think of something makes us think of it more[1]. More suffering instead of less. Ongoing emotional suppression can also add to mental health issues such as OCD, depression, and addiction. Headaches, IBS, asthma, high blood pressure, heart disease, diabetes, and a compromised immune system are other problems associated with trying to push down difficult feelings over the long term.

We need the full range of our experience in order to feel whole. Our feelings provide important information about what's going on around us, and how we're being treated. Do we sense danger? Perhaps we need to scoot. Delight? Confusion? We need to know. It might take practice to read our signals accurately if we've been harmed. For example, when I feel confused, sometimes I think that everyone else understands except me. Usually, however, it means that something doesn't add up. I'm always getting better at trusting my confusion.

Being in touch with our feelings also makes it easier to communicate effectively with others—easier to pick a restaurant, request

---

[1] Wegner, D. et al. (1987). Paradoxical effects of thought suppression. Journal of Personality and Social Psychology, 53(1), 5-13. http://dx.doi.org/10.1037/0022-3514.53.1.5

some alone time, or ask for a raise. How can our friends, loved ones, and associates understand us if we don't know ourselves? Plus, we will have more energy to give if our resources aren't tapped out trying to avoid emotional honesty.

Eventually I came to full agreement with my grandfather: presence of mind is worth even the most difficult struggles. We cannot live selective moments of our lives, and there is no peace while perpetually running from hurt. I suspect you might agree, because you're holding this journal.

So hang in there! Easy does it! With patience (lots of patience), overcoming hardship cultivates empathy, wisdom, and a sense of empowerment, all of which can be used to face challenges—and triumphs—more effectively with a clear head and full heart. These are the gifts of adversity available to us all.

Date and time:

I feel:

When I write:

Date and time:

I feel:

It's interesting:

Date and time:

I feel:

When I think about setting limits:

Date and time:

I feel:

When I was ten:

Date and time:

I feel:

The time of day I like best:

Date and time:

I feel:

I'm doing this because:

Date and time:

I feel:

Tuning in to my body:

Breathe-in experience, breathe-out poetry.

Muriel Rukeyser

Date and time:

I feel:

My non-negotiable needs:

Date and time:

I feel:

For me, money:

Date and time:

I feel:

Things I'm not responsible for:

Date and time:

I feel:

When I speak up:

Date and time:

I feel:

Three things that give me hope:

Date and time:

I feel:

When I'm alone:

Date and time:

I feel:

When I ask for help:

> *I know God will not give me anything I can't handle.*
> *I just wish that He didn't trust me so much.*
>
> Mother Teresa

Date and time:

I feel:

My dream vacation:

Date and time:

I feel:

A pleasant surprise:

Date and time:

I feel:

Three things I really love about my body:

Date and time:

I feel:

The person I wish I could tell:

Date and time:

I feel:

Something to celebrate:

Date and time:

I feel:

The qualities of someone I really admire:

Date and time:

I feel:

What's in my way?

Don't quit…Where there's life…There's hope.

Marcus Tullius Cicero

Date and time:

I feel:

I wish I hadn't told:

Date and time:

I feel:

Sex:

Date and time:

I feel:

It feels good in my body when:

Date and time:

I feel:

Don't try to tell me:

Date and time:

I feel:

It feels like I can never get back:

Date and time:

I feel:

It seems silly but:

Date and time:

I feel:

When I'm with a group of people:

> *At the center of your being you have the answer;*
> *you know who you are and you know what you want.*
>
> Lao Tzu

3

BUT WHAT DO I DO ABOUT IT?

As a therapist, I work with a lot of people who have been traumatized. I've been there, so I know it's not easy. Terrible events like rape ricochet through life, destroying today, shaking up the past, and leaving a question mark for the future. There's grief and rage. Family dynamics. So much to sort through, with such slow relief. In the middle of it all, when talking feels pointless, everyone wants to know *but what do I do about it?*

The frustrating answer is that gaining emotional insight, collecting information, and sharing stories *is* doing something. It's not everything, but it's the foundation. Knowing who we are and what's meaningful to us is the basis for a sense of security and fulfillment. Ideally, growing up provides lots of opportunity and support for discovering, trusting, and sharing our unique gifts and preferences. Childhood creates a blueprint for building our lives even as our specific interests change.

Trauma has a way of finding the cracks in our personal infrastructure and blasting them open. If early nurturing or circumstances have been less than adequate, trauma will widen the gap between *where I am* and *where I want to be* even further. It takes a lot of courage and patience (*who has patience at a time like this?!*) to get back on track.

There's nothing wrong with wanting to feel better quickly. The impulse to "do something" (*anything!*) originates from a place of self-love. Even potentially destructive activities such as drinking too much alcohol, overeating, or taking drugs begin as attempts to balance out pain or compensate for a feeling of deadness.

Hear that again: the origin of just about everything you do is an attempt to take care of yourself. Whether or not it's working is a different matter. Any behavior has the potential to hijack life rather than enhance it. Sometimes staying still is the hardest accomplishment, but the most helpful.

Taking action when there is none to take is sometimes a way to avoid feeling powerless in a world turned upside down by trauma. We pace like a tiger, agile, ready to pounce. Danger lurks around every unknown corner. Problems arise when it feels better to anticipate pain than expect good fortune, so we can't stop pacing.

The beautiful fact is: to grow is to transcend what we know. Sometimes the best preparation for the future is the miserable, unglamorous, moment right *now*. *Now* might land with a thud and refuse to budge. It might require tears, or anger. After sexual trauma, getting through the day heartbeat by heartbeat is a fine feat. When it's time to do something more, there's usually no need to ask "what?" The impulse will be strong, and it will feel true.

Until then, be kind to yourself. Practice paying attention to itty-bitty needs and desires. When you can stand it, sit still. Try not to fill up the empty places in your soul with somebody else's answers; use this journal to find your own. Trust where you are.

Date and time:

I feel:

If today were a book, the title would be:

Date and time:

I feel:

When I think about God:

Date and time:

I feel:

I would appreciate it if:

Date and time:

I feel:

I deserve happiness:

Date and time:

I feel:

Success means:

Date and time:

I feel:

It's easiest when:

Date and time:

I feel:

When it's hard to forgive myself:

To wish to be well is part of becoming well.

Seneca

Date and time:

I feel:

At my lowest point:

Date and time:

I feel:

My mother:

Date and time:

I feel:

Ways I've numbed myself:

Date and time:

I feel:

I know it's okay to:

Date and time:

I feel:

It's hard to admit, but:

Date and time:

I feel:

I've made some major strides:

Date and time:

I feel:

Three qualities I admire in myself:

Being entirely honest with oneself is good exercise.

Sigmund Freud

Date and time:

I feel:

Patience:

Date and time:

I feel:

Someone I really loved growing up:

Date and time:

I feel:

The way I'd describe myself:

Date and time:

I feel:

Chaos means:

Date and time:

I feel:

Taking care of others:

Date and time:

I feel:

I wish:

Date and time:

I feel:

My sleep habits:

Anger insists that we consider our circumstances and make adjustments.

The Year After

Date and time:

I feel:

When I was younger:

Date and time:

I feel:

The ways I cope:

Date and time:

I feel:

Creativity:

Date and time:

I feel:

I forgive myself for:

Date and time:

I feel:

Burnout warning signs:

Date and time:

I feel:

I know I feel because:

Date and time:

I feel:

How my spiritual life has changed:

---

*The Path that leadeth on is lighted by one fire—
the light of daring burning in the heart. The more one dares,
the more he shall obtain.*

Helena Blavatsky

Date and time:

I feel:

I have learned:

Date and time:

I feel:

When I feel good about myself:

Date and time:

I feel:

Happiness is:

Date and time:

I feel:

Sometimes I pretend:

Date and time:

I feel:

Telling my story:

Date and time:

I feel:

Today, my biggest challenge is:

Date and time:

I feel:

I've started to notice:

It is easy to be brave from a safe distance.

Aesop

Date and time:

I feel:

A few things I've always wanted to try:

Date and time:

I feel:

Do I feel connected to the child I was?

Date and time:

I feel:

It feeds my soul when:

Date and time:

I feel:

The wisest thing I've ever heard someone say:

Date and time:

I feel:

Something I learned the hard way:

Date and time:

I feel:

This is what makes me saddest:

Date and time:

I feel:

When I'm ready to give up:

> *If you bring forth what is within you, what you bring forth will save you.*
> *If you do not bring forth what is within you,*
> *what you do not bring forth will destroy you.*
>
> Gospel of Thomas

4

CREATIVE HEALING

Art is good for you. A study[2] published in the *American Journal of Public Health* reviewed literature on the healing effects of music, visual arts, and movement therapies, as well as expressive writing. The bottom line: dust of your tuba, put on your tap shoes. Grab a paint brush, open your journal. (Hey, you're already doing that. Yay!) The researchers found that creative therapies decrease stress, anxiety, and mood disturbances, and increase physical and psychological wellbeing—especially for those struggling with topics that are difficult to put into words.

Art functions on many levels. First, it's a diversion. Nothing wrong with a little distraction. Second, art gets us into the creative right brain and out of the analytical left brain, which will never make sense of something like sexual assault. Third, creative activities speak the "language" of the lower brain, which deals in images and gut reactions rather than words and thoughts to process sensory information. Even severe disturbances like PTSD can be soothed.

---

[2] Stuckey, H. L., & Nobel, J. (2010). The Connection Between Art, Healing, and Public Health: A Review of Current Literature. *American Journal of Public Health, 100*(2), 254–263. http://doi.org/10.2105/AJPH.2008.156497

When the brain and body continue to respond to a crisis that's long over, we call it posttraumatic stress disorder. The good news is, the same neurological wiring process that got the brain stuck in trauma mode can be reworked by positive events and activities. Engaging in complex new projects like making art improves communication between different parts of the brain and stimulates fresh neural connectivity, a fundamental component of lasting recovery. Research also indicates that creative endeavors decrease levels of the stress hormone cortisol,[3] and boost production of the feel-good hormone dopamine.[4]

I've included some of my favorite art therapy activities at the end of the journal. Turn to Creative Healing—Activities on page 355 anytime. You certainly don't need to be an artist to benefit; put your judgment on hold and let your soul play. The projects should be pleasant, even fun. See if you can find a flow state—feel the surge of energy and joy. Do you notice any changes in your sense of mastery, safety, and resilience? If so, do the feelings carry over into the rest of your life, even for a short time?

I'd love to hear how it's going! Feel free to send an email or visit me on Facebook or Goodreads.

---

[3] Kaimal, G., Ray, K., & Muniz, J.M. (2016 forthcoming) Outcomes of visual self-expression: Changes in cortisol and narratives of self-perceived impact. *Art Therapy: Journal of the American Art Therapy Association.*

[4] Ishizu T, Zeki S (2011) Toward A Brain-Based Theory of Beauty. PLoS ONE 6(7): e21852. doi:10.1371/journal.pone.0021852

Date and time:

I feel:

The last time I laughed so much my sides hurt:

Date and time:

I feel:

I feel most alive when:

Date and time:

I feel:

I'm tired of everyone:

Date and time:

I feel:

If it wasn't too inconvenient:

Date and time:

I feel:

My financial goals:

Date and time:

I feel:

Something no one understands:

Date and time:

I feel:

I felt invisible when:

My life will be defined by my own actions, not yours.

The Year After

Date and time:

I feel:

Advice I'd give my younger self:

Date and time:

I feel:

I used to love to:

Date and time:

I feel:

One day:

Date and time:

I feel:

I'm most at peace when:

Date and time:

I feel:

Compassion:

Date and time:

I feel:

If I had more energy:

Date and time:

I feel:

I know I'm not alone:

Nothing endures but change.

Heraclitus

Date and time:

I feel:

Suffering:

Date and time:

I feel:

My true purpose:

Date and time:

I feel:

The ways I used to cope:

Date and time:

I feel:

I felt best about myself when:

Date and time:

I feel:

I can't live without:

Date and time:

I feel:

If my body could talk:

Date and time:

I feel:

The words I most want to hear:

I was always looking outside myself for strength and confidence, but it comes from within. It is there all the time.

Anna Freud

Date and time:

I feel:

It's time to say no to:

Date and time:

I feel:

When I'm older:

Date and time:

I feel:

An obstacle I can overcome:

Date and time:

I feel:

Grief:

Date and time:

I feel:

Living on the edge:

Date and time:

I feel:

A burning question:

Date and time:

I feel:

People who need me:

My true being is unborn and changeless.

Krishna

Date and time:

I feel:

My first love:

Date and time:

I feel:

It brings tears to my eyes:

Date and time:

I feel:

Vulnerability:

Date and time:

I feel:

My happiest memory:

Date and time:

I feel:

Something I need more of:

Date and time:

I feel:

Do I believe in miracles?

Date and time:

I feel:

My intuition:

No snowflake ever falls in the wrong place.

Zen Proverb

5

Sex

I've listened to a lot of stories about rape through the years—as a survivor in my own support group, as a rape crisis advocate, and as a therapist and author. Let me assure you: there are many different reactions to intimacy in the aftermath of sexual violence. None are wrong, all are understandable. Here are some common themes in composite form to protect privacy. In other words, these are mash-ups of comments made by various women rather than direct quotes from specific people. Details have also been altered to ensure anonymity.

I was overcome with guilt when I started feeling sexy again. I also felt like I was betraying some unwritten girl code when I was attracted to a guy for the first time after my rape. Shouldn't I hate penises now?

I became really promiscuous after I was raped. I figured the guy was going to have sex with me whether I wanted to or not; I might as well be the one in charge.

I couldn't look at my body in the mirror for a long time. I still don't like to look. And I like the lights out.

I used my rape as punishment for being a lesbian for years. My family did, too. It's taken a long time to feel proud of who I am, much less sexy. I'm with an amazing, supportive partner now, and she's not going anywhere!

One time my boyfriend thought it would be really sexy to wake me up by going down on me. It really backfired. I was abused by my stepbrother, who'd sneak into my room at night when I was a kid, so that's not the way I want to wake up. I freaked out. I felt bad, but don't ever try to surprise me like that.

The first time I tried to have sex after I was raped, I started crying and shaking as soon as I took off my pants. I got dressed again and ran out the door. The guy texted me and called, but I never got back to him. I felt too embarrassed.

I didn't even masturbate for a year. I had absolutely no sexual appetite. Sex felt dirty.

I did a lot of masturbating. It's the only way I could get off for a long time. It's still difficult to "let go" and have an orgasm with someone else present.

My girlfriend and I were both raped. She was abused by her older cousin when she was 10, and I was raped in college by a "friend." It's great when we can both lose ourselves in the moment, but it's tricky. Often either she's triggered, or I am....it sucks.

I really love sex. I lost my virginity to rape and I feel bad for being such a sexual person, but I am.

I didn't think too much about my rape after the initial chaos—until my daughter got to be a tween. Now I worry about her—probably more than is normal. I don't want her to experience what I went through. We talk about sex and safety a lot.

I could easily live without sex.

I'm sick of having the "rape talk" before I have sex with a new partner. But it's part of what makes me feel safe. If he can't handle it, I shouldn't have sex with him.

Sometimes I feel sick after sex. I mean, one time I actually threw up.

I've never told anyone I've slept with what happened to me. I think it would make it harder to forget.

My boyfriend was supportive for a long time, but then one night he told me he couldn't handle our "f'd up" sex life. He was really angry and stormed out of my apartment. I actually felt heartbroken for him, although I should probably have felt heartbroken for me. The relationship didn't last.

I was raped 17 years ago in the park near my house. I was newly married at the time, and I'm still with my husband. Our sex life really took a hit, but we worked at it. Thankfully, he was really patient. Not perfect, but patient. Otherwise, I don't know what would have happened.

I don't think about my rape much anymore. Sex is fine. Occasionally, memories will distract me, but usually it's a non-issue.

Do you identify with any of these statements? Is there something that needs to be added to this list?

Date and time:

I feel:

The song I can listen to over and over:

Date and time:

I feel:

I most resent:

Date and time:

I feel:

The most outrageous thing I've ever done:

Date and time:

I feel:

Nobody knows that:

Date and time:

I feel:

As a child, I hoped that:

Date and time:

I feel:

The biggest lie I ever told:

Date and time:

I feel:

The most courageous thing I've ever done:

We know what we are, but know not what we may be.

William Shakespeare

Date and time:

I feel:

My confidence:

Date and time:

I feel:

I can't stop thinking about:

Date and time:

I feel:

I'd most like to meet:

Date and time:

I feel:

My favorite childhood toy/game:

Date and time:

I feel:

If money were no object:

Date and time:

I feel:

Must-have qualities in a romantic partner:

Date and time:

I feel:

A perfect day:

Being present in our hurt is necessary if we are to also be present in our joy.

The Year After

Date and time:

I feel:

I feel guilty about:

Date and time:

I feel:

What do I need today?

Date and time:

I feel:

My thoughts about psychotherapy:

Date and time:

I feel:

I most dread:

Date and time:

I feel:

When I look back on this time, I imagine I'll:

Date and time:

I feel:

Something I must do during my lifetime:

Date and time:

I feel:

I never thought I'd say this:

No man ever steps in the same river twice, for it's not the same river and he's not the same man.

Heraclitus

Date and time:

I feel:

Something in my life I need to let go of:

Date and time:

I feel:

It's disappointing:

Date and time:

I feel:

Three things I take delight in:

Date and time:

I feel:

I wish I had spoken up when:

Date and time:

I feel:

What it means to have a healthy sense of self-esteem:

Date and time:

I feel:

Something I disagree with about my upbringing:

Date and time:

I feel:

Is there anyone I need to release?

> *Above the cloud with it's shadow, is the star with its light.*
> *Above all things, reverence thyself.*
>
> Pythagoras

Date and time:

I feel:

Breathing deeply:

Date and time:

I feel:

Something I want to see before I die:

Date and time:

I feel:

My favorite photograph:

Date and time:

I feel:

The music that most uplifts me:

Date and time:

I feel:

A moment of transcendence:

Date and time:

I feel:

I'm thinking about, but not quite ready to:

Date and time:

I feel:

The person I'm most proud of:

Some of us think holding on makes us strong, but sometimes it is letting go.

Hermann Hesse

Date and time:

I feel:

It's unbearable:

Date and time:

I feel:

I tend to avoid:

Date and time:

I feel:

I wish someone had taught me:

Date and time:

I feel:

Three things I'm grateful for:

Date and time:

I feel:

When I'm quiet:

Date and time:

I feel:

Starting right now:

Date and time:

I feel:

I never knew it could hurt:

Self love is the instrument of our preservation.

Voltaire

6

FIGHT, FLIGHT, *FREEZE*

We humans are amazing, aren't we? We've built cities and empires. There is art so beautiful it makes you ache. Have you ever seen Michelangelo's Pietà? Or the Taj Mahal at sunrise? Technology has connected the globe—from the Arab Spring to my living room in autumn. I have a standing Spanish lesson with Mariana, even though she moved back to Buenos Aires.

We're also mammals. In spite of our sophisticated capabilities, animal instincts are powerful within us—especially during times of peril. Fight or flight, the unconscious survival reactions regulated by the sympathetic nervous system in response to danger, are well known. There is another physiological reaction, one that is much more common during sexual assault. Research shows that up to 50 percent of rape victims *freeze*[5]. Freezing is also a mammalian, autonomic response to danger.

During a traumatic event such as rape, our brains become very

---

[5] Campbell, R. (2012). The neurobiology of sexual assault [transcript]. Retrieved from http://nij.gov/multimedia/presenter/presenter-campbell/pages/presenter-campbell-transcript.aspx

busy[6]. A few of the key regions that get involved are the hypothalamus, located above the brain stem; the pituitary gland just below the hypothalamus; and the adrenals, which are on top of each kidney. The hypothalamus is like the Grand Central Station of the body because virtually all information passes through it on the way to the cortex, which is the thought and action part of the brain. The hypothalamus connects the sights, sounds, tastes, and emotions of the nervous system with the endocrine system.

The endocrine system is the collection of all the glands of the body, responsible for producing hormones that regulate metabolism, growth, and reactions to stress. The pituitary gland is the master gland. It makes its own hormones and influences the production of others. During an assault, the pituitary is in close communication with the adrenal gland. The hypothalamus signals to the pituitary gland, which alerts the adrenals that a traumatic thing is happening to the body.

Answering to the trauma, the adrenals release four main chemicals to help the body cope: catecholamine—adrenaline—prepares the body to fight or fly. Cortisol, the steroid hormone, produces energy. Opiods, a kind of natural morphine, deal with pain, and oxytocin helps soothe emotional distress.

The flood of hormones has other effects. Adrenaline impairs rational thought. Opiods, which remain in the body for as long as 96 hours after an assault, flatten out emotions into a zombie-like expression. In contrast, oxytocin injects feel-good chemicals into the mix. The net result of this intense neurophysiological activity is rapid-cycling mood swings that are as confusing to the traumatized person as to everyone else. Last but not least, corticosteroids, activated at super-high levels to deal with major crises like sexual assault, can cause a complete shutdown of the body. Shut. Down. This is the freeze response.

The technical term for hormone-fueled paralysis is "tonic immobility." Just like a wild animal playing dead to put off its prey, a

---

[6] Kozlowska, K., et al. (2015). Fear and the defense cascade: Clinical implications and management. *Harvard Review of Psychiatry*, 23(4), 263-287.

human being may freeze as an evolutionary response to attack or threat of attack. Rape-induced paralysis can happen if the assailant is a stranger or a so-called friend. It can be triggered by a subtle tingle of apprehension or by the shift from *maybe* to the panic of realizing there's no choice. What's more, being aware of a frozen state does nothing to reverse the reaction, which might last a few moments or much, much longer.

In other words, "just lying there" doesn't imply consent. Or weakness. Not fighting back is no comment on character. Inaction indicates having a freeze response—being unable to move arms or legs, torso, hands, or pinkie toe. This isn't a reaction anyone has control over. It's an unconscious, instinctive response to danger developed since caveman time. It kicks in instantaneously, long before our thinking brains catch up.

Bodies are built to guide us to the best means of survival in any given circumstance. Sometimes fleeing is possible. Most often, however, freezing is what happens to sexual assault victims. Plus a jumbled post-rape brain swimming in chemicals. Police officers, district attorneys, and judges need to understand these processes. As do university personnel. Friends and family. The media. It's time to stop holding victims responsible for the crimes committed against them when they most need our love and support.

Date and time:

I feel:

For me, desire:

Date and time:

I feel:

My dream home:

Date and time:

I feel:

If I wasn't afraid of hurting someone's feelings:

Date and time:

I feel:

The best job I ever had:

Date and time:

I feel:

Sometimes I worry it's too late:

Date and time:

I feel:

Something I'm really good at:

Date and time:

I feel:

I was jealous:

Victim-blaming is an attempt to hold on to the fantasy "it could never happen to me."

The Year After

Date and time:

I feel:

I never admitted to anyone:

Date and time:

I feel:

My first memory:

Date and time:

I feel:

The clothes I love most:

Date and time:

I feel:

A perfect day:

Date and time:

I feel:

The way I show people I care:

Date and time:

I feel:

In five years' time:

Date and time:

I feel:

I never knew:

And the day came when the risk to remain tight in a bud was more painful than the risk it took to blossom.

Anaïs Nin

Date and time:

I feel:

These things I know:

Date and time:

I feel:

Prayer:

Date and time:

I feel:

I make a lot of noise when:

Date and time:

I feel:

Trust:

Date and time:

I feel:

How do I handle conflict?

Date and time:

I feel:

My biggest treasure:

Date and time:

I feel:

When I'm bored:

Poetry is when an emotion has found its thought and the thought has found words.
The best way out is always through.

Robert Frost

Date and time:

I feel:

The place I live:

Date and time:

I feel:

Children:

Date and time:

I feel:

My most satisfying meltdown:

Date and time:

I feel:

When I can't sleep:

Date and time:

I feel:

To whom am I a blessing?

Date and time:

I feel:

Holidays mean:

Date and time:

I feel:

I'd love to explore:

Because you are alive, everything is possible.

Thich Nhat Hanh

Date and time:

I feel:

My personality:

Date and time:

I feel:

I was embarrassed when:

Date and time:

I feel:

Empathy means:

Date and time:

I feel:

I'm most like:

Date and time:

I feel:

No matter what anyone says:

Date and time:

I feel:

My favorite splurge:

Date and time:

I feel:

My untapped talent:

There is a place for anger. Anger is a lifelong gauge that alerts us to harm.

The Year After

7

MEMORY AND RAPE

Memory is another neurological function bossed around by trauma[7]. Two of the big brain structures that are involved, the amygdala and hippocampus, are located deep within the temporal lobe. They're part of the limbic system, which deals with survival instincts. The amygdala regulates heartbeat and other fundamental functions, while the hippocampus is the body's front line in processing fear. All emotions, from disgust to elation, pity or pride; and drives such as hunger, sex, or dominance are controlled by the limbic system. The amygdala and hippocampus are also involved with memory.

Through a process called encoding, the hippocampus is an excellent personal assistant. It makes note of all sensory details, gets organized, and stores everything. This information can then become consolidated, or part of long-term memory. However, both the amygdala, which provides the initial, emotional memory, and the hippocampus, which sorts through everything, are extremely sensitive to

---

[7] Campbell, R. (2012). The neurobiology of sexual assault [transcript]. Retrieved from http://nij.gov/multimedia/presenter/presenter-campbell/pages/presenter-campbell-transcript.aspx
Sherin, J.E. and Nemeroff, C. E. (2011). Post-traumatic stress disorder: The neurobiological impact of psychological trauma. *Dialogues in Clinical Neuroscience*, 13(3), 263-278.

hormonal shifts. The surge of adrenaline, opioids, cortisol, and oxytocin that are released during sexual assault utterly destroys the ability of these brain structures to make sense of anything. Much less encode and consolidate the experience.

The result of disturbed hippocampal processing is fragmented and poorly organized memories that are difficult to retrieve. Memory after rape has been likened to notes on bits of paper that have been scattered all over the place—even stuffed into unlikely places like the pencil sharpener[8]. No wonder it's tough to give a coherent report in the aftermath of trauma. But this is interesting: unless alcohol or other substances have added to memory disturbance, the information on those bits of paper are mostly accurate. Just jumbled.

Brains flooded with hormones, confused, and preoccupied with survival, shouldn't be expected to do the impossible. A rape victim's disorganized report is not an indication of lying. Nor are emotions that seem out of sync with a terrible ordeal. If anything, these reactions support rather than negate the occurrence of sexual assault. An insensitive interviewer will make matters worse. The more doubting or hostile he or she is, the more discombobulated a traumatized person becomes. Suspiciousness is perceived as another threat, which it is—a threat to protection, integrity, and justice.

It's a no brainer: people who work with sexual assault survivors need special training. Understanding the neurobiology of trauma is a priority for sensitive, survivor-centered care. Not to mention improved justice. When victims expect to be treated with respect, they are more likely to report sexual violence. If reports are taken seriously, more criminals may be stopped. Win—win.

Knowing brain basics is also compassionate self-care. We are highly sophisticated and instinctive creatures, with internal systems developed through the ages. Reactions that seem odd are usually body

---

[8] Campbell, R. (2012). The neurobiology of sexual assault [transcript]. Retrieved from http://nij.gov/multimedia/presenter/presenter-campbell/pages/presenter-campbell-transcript.aspx

and mind at work to find balance. It helps when we can cut ourselves some slack. I know. Easier said than done.

Date and time:

I feel:

Support groups:

Date and time:

I feel:

In my circle of friends, it's well known that:

Date and time:

I feel:

Intimacy:

Date and time:

I feel:

What I can depend on:

Date and time:

I feel:

I have agency over:

Date and time:

I feel:

My views on religion:

Date and time:

I feel:

Even though I know it's wrong:

> *Everybody needs beauty as well as bread, places to play in and pray in, where nature may heal and give strength to body and soul alike.*
>
> John Muir

Date and time:

I feel:

I revel in:

Date and time:

I feel:

If I were to give a talk, it would be about:

Date and time:

I feel:

It's devastating:

Date and time:

I feel:

I'm misunderstood when:

Date and time:

I feel:

Drugs and alcohol:

Date and time:

I feel:

Loss:

Date and time:

I feel:

My sexuality:

Time is the wisest counselor of all.

Pericles

Date and time:

I feel:

Some thoughts and feelings don't match:

Date and time:

I feel:

A triumph:

Date and time:

I feel:

As soon as I'm able:

Date and time:

I feel:

My father:

Date and time:

I feel:

Something I notice about humankind:

Date and time:

I feel:

The difference between anxiety and excitement:

Date and time:

I feel:

It never fails:

This above all: to thine own self be true.

William Shakespeare

Date and time:

I feel:

Social issues that concern me:

Date and time:

I feel:

To have a sense of entitlement:

Date and time:

I feel:

Meditation:

Date and time:

I feel:

If I were a world leader:

Date and time:

I feel:

I'm ready to forgive myself for:

Date and time:

I feel:

It's not an excuse:

Date and time:

I feel:

I felt abandoned when:

May the stars carry your sadness away,
may the flowers fill your heart with beauty,
may hope forever wipe away your tears,
and, above all, may silence make you strong.
Native American Proverb

Date and time:

I feel:

I should care, but I just don't:

Date and time:

I feel:

Items I'd put in a time capsule to be opened in 50 years:

Date and time:

I feel:

I finally understand:

Date and time:

I feel:

I time I felt shamed:

Date and time:

I feel:

It seems like just yesterday:

Date and time:

I feel:

My hero/heroine:

Date and time:

I feel:

I wish I could have said it better:

> He who would learn to fly one day must first learn to stand and walk and run and climb and dance; one cannot fly into flying.
>
> Friedrich Nietzsche

8

CREATIVE HEALING—DANCE AND MUSIC

When I'm out salsa dancing, the benefits of physical exercise, mental flexibility, and joy come together in a tour de force of healing. Kinesthetic, logical, musical, and emotional brain functions are activated in dance. Neuronal synapses, which are the ways information travels in the brain, become increasingly complex. Translation: I feel better. I've got more avenues to tackle challenges, and there's opportunity to rewire my brain for health. A recent study found that the kind of dance involving learning new steps, thinking, and making choices is more powerful for improving mental health than all other physical and mental activities studied[9]. Playing music came in second.

Timing, balance, and the way our body feels in space are key components of dance. As messages travel back and forth between the brain and muscles via the sensorimotor system, we get constant updates about internal and external sensations. This information provides the brain with a detailed map of our corporeal kingdom. Self-awareness is important for a sense of stability and personal agency. Just like knowing many words makes it easier to tell your best friend exactly how you want to decorate your new apartment, greater bodily awareness enhances

---

[9] Verghese, J, et al. (2003). Leisure activities and the risk of dementia in the elderly. *New England Journal of Medicine*, 348, 2508-2516.

feelings of vitality. You've got to have the lay of the land to feel safe and rule.

Dance and music also affect pulse rate, skin response, and blood pressure as the body matches tempo with the music[10]. Different types of music stimulate different emotions through specific brain circuits, with increased signaling in the endocrine system—the collection of glands in the body that produce hormones. The "stress circuit" made up of the hypothalamus, pituitary, and adrenal gland is called the HPA axis. It's a part of the endocrine system that plays a big role in neurological response to trauma like rape. Dance helps soothe this circuit, which sometimes has trouble calming down after a big shock[11].

The emotional and reward centers in the brain and body that are activated in crisis—and dance—impact levels of serotonin, dopamine, and oxytocin. Serotonin, most of which is stored in the gut, is the "feel important" hormone regulating inhibition. Dopamine, the "feel good" hormone, increases desire and is released by the hypothalamus. Oxytocin, the "relationship hormone" secreted by the pituitary gland, is involved with connection and trust. In addition to balancing crises reactions, dance combats anxiety, depression, and increases overall motivation[12].

There's more. Partner dancing fosters kinesthetic empathy[13]—

---

[10] Sakamoto, H. (2002). Psycho-circulatory responses caused by listening to music, and exposure to fluctuation noise or steady noise. *The Journal of Sound and Vibration*, 250(1), 23-29

[11] Jeong, Y., et al. (2005). Dance movement therapy improves emotional responses and modulates neurohormones in adolescents with mild depression. *International Journal of Neuroscience*, 115:1711-1720.

[12] Koch, S. et al. (2007). The joy dance: specific effects of a single dance intervention on psychiatric patients with depression. *The Arts in Psychotherapy*, 34: 340–349

[13] John Martin, *Introduction to the Dance* (New York: Dance Horizons, 1939).

heightened embodied understanding of the other, which leads to empathy more generally. The experience of learning a specific dance also creates neurological connections between dancers. As people learn movements together, they are creating shared perspectives and new tools for relating. A part of the left hemisphere of the cerebral cortex called Broca's area is responsible for language. Its mirror location in the right hemisphere is activated when we dance, supporting the notion that we are indeed communicating[14].

The right-brain, symbolic kind of communication that takes over during dance puts us in a creative state of mind. Primed to see connections and nuances, our emotional, expressive side tunes in to what the left-brain—concerned with absolutes and certainty—alone would miss. As a result, dance combats the frustrating tendency to fall back on familiar, if disturbed, thought patterns and behaviors, which are especially compelling during times of trauma.

Dance also takes advantage of the brain's "plasticity"[15]. This ability to constantly adjust in response to external influences allows unhelpful, entrenched reactions to be "rewired." The kind of dance that involves thinking, "listening," and responding quickly to a partner is especially helpful. It boosts brainpower, and beefs up neural pathways. The creation of new neural pathways and the repair of damaged ones is key to living stress-free, as well as minimizing cognitive decline as we age.

Everyone is wired for rhythmic movement and music. In fact, some of the brain centers involved are thought to be very old in terms of evolution. The amygdala—an almond-shaped structure deep in the

---

[14] Parsons, L. and Brown, S. "The Neuroscience of Dance." Retrieved from the internet on September 23, 2016. https://dantzan.eus/edukiak/the-neuroscience-of-dance

[15] Gazzaniga, M. S. (2008). Arts and cognition: Findings hint at relationships. In Carolyn Asbury and Barbara Rich (Eds.) *Learning, Arts, and the Brain; The Dana Consortium report on arts and cognition.* New York/Washington, D.C.: Dana Press

brain—is also associated with memory, emotion, and decision-making. The hippocampus—the most ancient part of the cerebral cortex—is correlated with spatial orientation, learning, memory, and emotion. Dance and music evolved to promote desire, bonding, communication, and trust—crucial for the survival of earth's earliest humans. To this day, all cultures have rituals related to dance and music. Even new babies respond to melodic sound, and infants as young as five months old begin to move their bodies to the beat.

 Think of dance and music as a powerful medicine for your soul. Enjoy the benefits until you're very, very old.

Date and time:

I feel:

My favorite book:

Date and time:

I feel:

A lost opportunity:

Date and time:

I feel:

Kissing:

Date and time:

I feel:

A small gift I could treat myself with:

Date and time:

I feel:

What in my life is abundant?

Date and time:

I feel:

A task I need to get to work on:

Date and time:

I feel:

The universe:

Every day in every way I am getting better and better.

Emile Coue

Date and time:

I feel:

How I want to be treated:

Date and time:

I feel:

Do I inhabit my body?

Date and time:

I feel:

What is it like to feel empowered?

Date and time:

I feel:

Acceptance:

Date and time:

I feel:

I've earned:

Date and time:

I feel:

Feelings that don't seem to go together, but do:

Date and time:

I feel:

At my next family gathering:

> *We cannot live in a world that is not our own,*
> *in a world that is interpreted for us by others.*
> *An interpreted world is not a home.*
>
> Hildegard of Bingen

Date and time:

I feel:

It's fleeting, but:

Date and time:

I feel:

Something I no longer want to make excuses for:

Date and time:

I feel:

My dreams:

Date and time:

I feel:

I really stepped up when:

Date and time:

I feel:

A good habit of mine:

Date and time:

I feel:

The deceptively simple act of listening:

Date and time:

I feel:

Persistence:

Pain is never permanent.

Teresa of Avila

Date and time:

I feel:

A conversation that changed my life:

Date and time:

I feel:

Thank you:

Date and time:

I feel:

Stillness:

Date and time:

I feel:

A friendly interaction that left a lasting impression:

Date and time:

I feel:

My favorite place to be in the rain:

Date and time:

I feel:

Moments of coincidence:

Date and time:

I feel:

A time I followed my own instincts:

---

*When we make sense of things,
even our most devastating challenges serve to empower us.*

The Year After

9

IT'S NOT EASY TO REPORT RAPE. HERE'S WHY.

1. Victims fear their reports won't be believed. Sometimes they're right—especially when a so-called friend or acquaintance is the rapist, which describes 38% of assaults. Many people feel that not being believed is a trauma second only to the rape itself. I've heard more than one survivor say that being doubted is worse. Says a lot, doesn't it?

Research over the past 20 years has taught us much about the profile of a sexual perpetrator. Few truths are more unsettling than the fact that rapists walk among us sometimes. When the offender is someone who was trusted, the impact is most devastating. It's easier for some people to degrade the victim than lose a sense of security within their community.

2. Reporting sexual assault can be re-traumatizing even with state-of-the-art care. Thankfully, we've seen great improvements in victim-centered treatment since the introduction of the Violence Against Women Act (VAWA) in 1994. There has been increased training for police officers and medical staff. Rape crisis advocates exist to offer support and guide new victims through choices including whether to report or not. We know much more about the physiology of trauma.

Nevertheless, reporting under the best of circumstances requires telling and re-telling of painful and confusing events. Everyone needs to know the details: doctors, nurses, law enforcement, and many others should prosecution proceed. Also, forensic medical exams are unpleasant and intrusive, though important (so important!)

3. Victims believe their sexual assault is not serious enough to report. Sad but true. In fact, the FBI ranks rape second only to murder on the index of violent crime, whether or not a weapon was used or physical injuries were sustained during an assault. Sometimes rape is number 1 because killing can happen by mistake, while rape is never an accident.

Rape is a crime of power and control, more often than not perpetrated by serial offenders who are masterful in manipulation. Such rapists are skilled in victimizing the most vulnerable, preying on their insecurities, and exerting the least amount of force necessary to get their way. The use of drugs and alcohol serves both to minimize resistance and impair memory, introducing doubt into victims' minds as well as those who might hear their reports.

4. Victims fear retaliation if they report. It is typical to feel unsafe in a world turned upside down by trauma—what once was sure and true is no longer dependable. When the rapist is known, terror of being violated again or harassed in other ways is multiplied. The rapists of a young woman I know followed her around her college campus month after month, lurking in doorways and across the dining hall. The message was silent but clear: report, and we know where to find you.

5. Victims fear having intimate details of their lives revealed publically. Many rape cases end with a plea agreement out of court, but if a case goes to trial, the victim may have to testify. There now exist some legal tools to prevent prior sexual history and other irrelevant personal information from entering the record (hooray again, VAWA!) Nevertheless, the process of testifying can be taxing. Another reason why a measly 3% of rapists ever serve a day in jail.

It should be empowering to name criminals and seek justice, not humiliating. To that end, we must ensure that allegations of sexual violence are taken seriously and investigated thoroughly—for the good of everyone involved. We must also accept that rapists are usually not masked strangers; they exist on all levels of the social strata.

In the end, the process of reporting and prosecuting sexual crime is more than one victim's triumph. It's a service to the entire community. Because most rapists are repeat offenders, a conviction carries lasting impact. It just may prevent someone else from being harmed.

Date and time:

I feel:

What does commitment mean to me?

Date and time:

I feel:

A difficult moment handled gracefully:

Date and time:

I feel:

Memories of my favorite childhood teacher:

Date and time:

I feel:

Who am I becoming?

Date and time:

I feel:

Do I pay attention?

Date and time:

I feel:

A mistake that was a blessing in disguise:

Date and time:

I feel:

I long for:

The best thing one can do when it's raining is to let it rain.

Henry Wadsworth Longfellow

Date and time:

I feel:

How do I experience time?

Date and time:

I feel:

My house:

Date and time:

I feel:

What surprises me about where I am?

Date and time:

I feel:

A time I was alone but not lonely:

Date and time:

I feel:

An unexpected moment of generosity:

Date and time:

I feel:

For me, freedom:

Date and time:

I feel:

Aggression vs. assertiveness:

I'm not afraid of storms, for I'm learning to sail my ship.

Louisa May Alcott

Date and time:

I feel:

A time I felt special:

Date and time:

I feel:

My greatest fear:

Date and time:

I feel:

Ecstasy:

Date and time:

I feel:

The biggest lie I've told myself:

Date and time:

I feel:

A kindness I'll never forget:

Date and time:

I feel:

Clever ways I've survived:

Date and time:

I feel:

How a sense of empowerment is communicated:

We acquire the strength we have overcome.

Ralph Waldo Emerson

Date and time:

I feel:

My support system:

Date and time:

I feel:

What is it time to reevaluate?

Date and time:

I feel:

The nurturing I received as a child:

Date and time:

I feel:

Is the glass half empty or half full?

Date and time:

I feel:

Evidence of abundance in my life:

Date and time:

I feel:

It's a delicate balance:

Date and time:

I feel:

I seek greater clarity:

Although we cannot change the past, we can stake our claim on it and make it ours. We can know for ourselves where we have been and use that wisdom to build our future.

The Year After

Date and time:

I feel:

How do I best recharge my energies?

Date and time:

I feel:

I've made allowances for:

Date and time:

I feel:

I felt like a burden:

Date and time:

I feel:

What gets in the way of self-care?

Date and time:

I feel:

I felt sexy:

Date and time:

I feel:

A time I knew best after all:

Date and time:

I feel:

It's complicated:

Do not lose hope, nor be sad. You will surely be victorious if you are true in Faith.

The Quran

Date and time:

I feel:

Forgiveness?

Date and time:

I feel:

What it's like to put myself first:

Date and time:

I feel:

`What do I make harder than it needs to be?

Date and time:

I feel:

The silliest thing about me:

Date and time:

I feel:

My dream job:

Date and time:

I feel:

A secret I was asked to keep:

Date and time:

I feel:

Hatred:

Better than a thousand hollow words, is one word that brings peace.

Buddha

10

HOW TO HELP SOMEONE WHO'S BEEN SEXUALLY ASSAULTED WITHOUT MAKING THINGS WORSE

I have to say, in the immediate aftermath of my sexual assault, I had excellent help. (I know this isn't everyone's story.) Kind, respectful paramedics and an emergency room with state-of-the-art sexual violence standards helped carry me through the first few hours. To this day, I remember the name of my nurse with fondness and gratitude.

Over the weeks that followed, many people rallied around me. Friends were always available to remind me to take my medications, to lend a shoulder to cry on, or a sofa to sleep on when I couldn't bear to be in my own apartment. They went with me to doctor's appointments and held my hand through the early process of participating in criminal prosecution after the rapist was identified in a lineup.

Eventually, the bruises around my neck from where the rapist had choked me into submission healed. I went back to my job waiting tables at an upscale restaurant. Assuming my life was more or less back to normal, friends and family became less solicitous and were perplexed by my continued fatigue, growing irritability, and dark mood.

My dad figured I just needed a little cheering up. He came to visit from North Carolina and dragged me to museums, out to eat, to the park, to the Seaport. Spent before the day even began, my shoulders and back aching from the effort of being alive, I was far too exhausted to enjoy any of it. While he pored over lunch menus and subway maps, I tried but failed to fight off violent flashbacks of the assault.

There was that moment on the stairs. A confused feeling as I was swept up by the neck. I screamed. Then there was no more breath.

I didn't have the energy to tell him that that last thing I wanted to do was sightsee. Instead I snapped sarcastically, "Sure, let's go frolicking!" He took offense and answered, "You don't need to act all pissed off."

Then there was my roommate, who insisted on treating me to dinner when my birthday rolled around not long after the rape. Seated in a trendy restaurant at a time of night when I would have much rather been in bed, she encouraged me to splurge on whatever dishes I wanted—as if that could somehow erase or override what had happened. I felt like I was in a vat of petroleum jelly; half awake, with no appetite whatsoever. Still, I ordered and ate, nodding politely without tasting a thing as she complimented me on my hair.

When my spirits still hadn't lifted some time later, she suggested I try scented candles or a bubble bath. About 16 weeks into the period I'd come to think of as *after*, she reminded me, "Everyone has problems, you know."

In both cases—as with colleagues who stopped asking how I was doing and friends who eventually stopped calling to check in—no harm was intended. Everyone was trying to help I their own way. Yet their efforts fell flat.

Most people simply couldn't imagine the depths of terror that continued to strike every time I heard a noise, a honk, or voice behind me on the street. No one could guess how acute the panic, anxiety, and anger still plaguing me were. The constant feeling that there was no more breath.

Nor, luckily, can most of us. As a result, it's extremely difficult to know how, exactly, to help somebody who's been raped. Our gut reaction about what to say in the aftermath of this tragedy can be far off-target. Sometimes what we say can even backfire, making the victim feel misunderstood and alone.

For example, telling a rape survivor to "stop thinking about it," or "try to move on" can send an unintentional message that something is wrong with the survivor for being preoccupied and hurt. When I was recovering, many of my friends' and family members' reactions left me feeling as if I'd been abandoned in the desert with a canteen and told to find my way back to civilization.

Today, with decades of hindsight including many years of training and experience as a psychotherapist, I understand the shock and utter devastation rape inflicts affects upon the psyche. I know that the impact stays with victims for a much longer time than many imagine.

It is not uncommon to experience symptoms such as anxiety or sadness for over a year, and to continue to remember and reflect on aspects of the event for many years to come. Thinking about what happened for prolonged periods of time is a normal reaction to trauma as the survivor works to integrate the experience into his or her life narrative. Recognizing and respecting this is the first step victims' friends and loved ones can take to lend support.

Another way to help is to assist with practical matters like grocery shopping, driving to doctor's appointments, or helping around the house. Helping out in small, practical ways offers invaluable material support while showing that you care—especially at a time when even simple tasks can be overwhelming.

Above all, friends and loved ones should simply try to listen. Let the survivor guide the conversation, making comments that acknowledge rather than dismiss the survivor's feelings, such as "I can certainly appreciate why you feel so lonely and afraid." Talking about what happened is instrumental to recovery, and feeling heard and understood is priceless.

Date and time:

I feel:

I define prosperity:

Date and time:

I feel:

What gets in the way of self-care?

Date and time:

I feel:

A moment to savor:

Date and time:

I feel:

I draw the line:

Date and time:

I feel:

Social media and me:

Date and time:

I feel:

I'm bursting with:

Date and time:

I feel:

Something it took a long time to give up:

Do I contradict myself?
Very well then I contradict myself,
(I am large, I contain multitudes.)

Walt Whitman

Date and time:

I feel:

I'm smart because:

Date and time:

I feel:

I'm inspired by:

Date and time:

I feel:

Shame vs. guilt:

Date and time:

I feel:

How I would speak to me if I were a child:

Date and time:

I feel:

My energies were depleted:

Date and time:

I feel:

A place that is magical to me:

Date and time:

I feel:

Why I may not be the burden I felt I was:

Our first and last love is self-love.

Christian Nestell Bovee

Date and time:

I feel:

A time I learned I was stronger than I thought:

Date and time:

I feel:

I'm unwilling to:

Date and time:

I feel:

My protector:

Date and time:

I feel:

A moment that popped my balloon:

Date and time:

I feel:

I felt sexy:

Date and time:

I feel:

I went out on a limb:

Date and time:

I feel:

The difference between "hurt" and "suffering":

> *The Lord is close to the brokenhearted*
> *and saves those who are crushed in spirit.*
>
> Psalm 34:18

Date and time:

I feel:

A gut reaction:

Date and time:

I feel:

My most beloved pet:

Date and time:

I feel:

A time I felt especially generous:

Date and time:

I feel:

What is enough?

Date and time:

I feel:

If you knew me better:

Date and time:

I feel:

An extraordinary circumstance:

Date and time:

I feel:

Why the way I feel makes a lot of sense:

By my love and my hope I beseech you—do not forsake hero in your soul!

Zarathustra

Date and time:

I feel:

The love of my life:

Date and time:

I feel:

Believe me:

Date and time:

I feel:

A turning point:

Date and time:

I feel:

A delightful mystery:

Date and time:

I feel:

The next item on my to do list:

Date and time:

I feel:

My tender heart:

Date and time:

I feel:

My authentic life:

Act as if what you do makes a difference. It does.

William James

11

Summing Up/ Looking Ahead

One thing's for certain: you are not the same person today as when you began this journal. The process of panning for nuggets of wisdom from life's harsh lessons cannot help but bring transformation. You feel more deeply, think a little differently. Because the way we think and feel affects how we interact with the world, which impacts what we get back, no doubt you've experienced change. I hope you're feeling safer. More grounded. Content.

What do you understand about yourself that you didn't know when you began this journal? Have questions been answered, new ones asked? Can you name your strengths? Are there areas for improvement? What do you like, what do you want?

Healing is a dynamic process, as is simply, "living." The practice of checking in with ourselves regularly never stops being useful. Necessary. *How do I feel? What do I think?* Paying attention to our own senses can take practice, especially when we we've been silenced by trauma. Keep at it. Therein lies counsel for our decisions.

Perhaps you are still struggling. That's okay. Everyone has her own process and pace. Healing is not a race, and life is not a direct course to a finish line. (I have to remind myself of this regularly. *Slow down, Ashley. Why are you rushing? Enjoy the ride.)*

Of course, it's easier to have patience when you're not hurting. It's difficult to recognize growth when you're feeling low. If you're inclined, take another pass through the daily prompts and art projects. No doubt you will find your responses different than before. You are evolving. Promise.

As for me, the date that marked the one-year anniversary of my rape passed without much ado. I bought myself a cupcake, wrote in my journal about how proud I felt for braving the most difficult year of my life, and carried on with the day. Gradually, my journal entries shifted from rape recovery to exploring new interests. I rediscovered my love of dance, and took classes in all sorts of things I'd always wanted to try. Judo and singing lessons didn't stick, but pottery sure did. I also found my way to a career I'm passionate about. I made new friends; fell in love, kept writing.

With the passage of time, rape stopped defining me. Although all of my experiences have shaped me, I no longer identified as a survivor, or even a "thriver." The shift happened naturally. What a gift. The greatest recovery of all is to live by our own design rather than in reaction to demons. Ironically, it's by confronting demons head-on that they gradually diminish.

In another twist, sexual violence is once again a prominent part of my life—this time by choice. My goal is for everyone to experience freedom from the haunting effects of trauma. In *The Year After* series, I offer my story and share what helped me. Although our paths are unique, there is usually enough common experience in rape recovery to bring comfort and hope. Let me know what you think.

I also invite you to stop by my Facebook page, where I post a lot about sexual violence recovery. Perhaps you'll even share a poem, or post pictures of your artistic creations. You're also welcome to visit me on Goodreads or send me an email.

In the meantime: Congratulations! You've come a long way!

Wishing you all the very best.

CREATIVE HEALING—ACTIVITIES

These are a few of my favorite art therapy techniques. They are in no particular order, so pick what interests you at any time.

It also might be interesting to work on an activity that doesn't immediately appeal to you. Does it teach you anything?

The projects are meant to be solo activities. They are designed to engage your senses and expand the deep, non-analytical part of your brain. Let yourself tune inward and find your flow. Enjoy.

1. Get yourself some finger paints, old newspaper, and put on a smock. Paint your mood while listening to music that fits. Getting messy is a bonus.

2. Make yourself a superhero cape. If you know how to sew, or love the craft store, feel free to get very fancy. If not, an old towel and magic markers will do. Draw on a big "S" for the superwoman that you are, or use your first initial. If you prefer, cut the letter out of fabric scraps and glue it on. Embellish the cape however you please with bows, buttons, whatever's lying around. Pin long ribbons (or knee-high socks) on two of the short corners so you can tie the cape around your neck. Wear it at every opportunity to feel extra powerful.

3. Rip or cut out images that appeal to you from old magazines. Collage what your ideal life looks like.

4. Take yourself on a photo expedition. Spend an hour or more in a park or other place of beauty photographing tiny things you have to look closely to see.

5. Make a postcard. Cut a piece of cardboard to the appropriate size and draw, collage, or decorate the front as if it were from your dream getaway destination. On the back, write a message from you-in-five-years to current you. Mail it to yourself if you can. If it's too private, keep it safe.

6. Dance! Often. Play upbeat music and turn it up. Loud. Wear

headphones if necessary. Move like you don't care about anything.

7. Head outside to find a rock that speaks to you. It can be big or small. Carry it home and paint it. Use nail polish if you don't have anything else. (Note to self: buy paint. Or nail polish.) What kind of message does the rock convey? Is it a touchstone or a weight? Maybe you'll keep it with you. Maybe you'll bury it. Maybe you'll toss it in a river with ceremony.

8. Color a mandala while listening to relaxing, soothing music. Visit colormandala.com or free-mandalas.net for free mandalas you can print out and color.

9. Make a mask. A paper plate is a fine base. Cut out eyes, nose, and mouth as you see fit. Decorate the outside to reflect how you imagine people see you. Decorate the inside to reflect how you see yourself.

10. Build your own website. You don't have to go live with it. Create pages on a topic that interests you or showcase your arts projects. Many website builders have free templates that are super easy to use—you don't have to be tech savvy at all. Really! Just a few examples are sitebuilder.com, weebly.com, or wix.com.

11. Collect some leaves. Write a prayer on each one with a pen. Scatter your prayers to the wind

12. Sing. Often and loudly. Look up the lyrics to your favorite songs, or better yet, make up the words spontaneously as you go along. Silly, angry, happy, let the songs reflect your mood. I like to do this alone in the car.

13. Using body paint, costume makeup, or regular makeup, paint your face and/or body as the angel, warrior, or magical creature that you are. Take some selfies.

14. Write an acrostic poem. What word most captures your mood right *now*? Write the word vertically and use each letter as the beginning of each line of the poem.

15. Get an inkpad and make fingerprint art. Tip: if you're right handed, ink up your left fingers so you can draw with your dominant hand. Or

ink your toes. Turn your prints into little creatures, flowers, or designs. Or whatever. Your creations will be as unique as your fingerprint.

16. Make music playlists. One with music that makes you feel powerful. Another with music that makes you feel hopeful. Another with music that makes you feel happy. Listen to them to help boost your mood.

This is by no means a complete list of healing arts activities. If you have other favorites, do share! I'd love to hear about them!

RESOURCES

National Teen Dating Abuse Helpline: **1-866-331-9474**
National Sexual Assault Hotline: **1-800-656-HOPE (4673)**
The National Suicide Helpline: **1-800-273-TALK (8255)**

Joyful Heart Foundation **joyfulheartfoundation.org** *"Our mission is to transform society's response to sexual assault, domestic violence, and child abuse, support survivors' healing, and end this violence forever."*

Men: **malesurvivor.org** *"Boys and men can be victims of sexual abuse and rape."*

Men Can Stop Rape **mencanstoprape.org** *"To mobilize men to use their strength for creating cultures free from violence, especially men's violence against women."*

Military Sexual Assault: **safehelpline.org** *"Sexual assault support for the DoD community."*

National Alliance to End Sexual Violence: **endsexualviolence.org** *"Its mission: to provide a missing voice in Washington for state coalitions and local programs advocating and organizing against sexual violence and for survivors."*

National Sexual Violence Resource Center: **nsvrc.org** *"Leaders in providing the latest resources on sexual violence."*

No More **nomore.org** *"Together we can end domestic violence and sexual assault."*

Promoting Awareness Victim Empowerment (PAVE) **pavingtheway.net** *"PAVE empowers students, parents, and civic leaders to end sexual violence with prevention education promoting respect of oneself and each other. Additionally, PAVE creates a safe space for survivors to thrive after trauma."*

Rape, Abuse, Incest National Network: **rainn.org** *"Rain is the nation's largest anti-sexual violence organization."*

SAFER: **safercampus.org** *"Strengthens student-led movements to combat sexual and interpersonal violence in campus communities."*

Scarleteen: **scarleteen.com** *"Sex ed for the real world."*

Teens: **loveisrespect.org** *"Loveisrespect's mission is to engage, educate and empower young people to prevent and end abusive relationships."*

Trauma Information Pages: **trauma-pages.com** *"The purpose of this award winning site is to provide information for clinicians and researchers in the traumatic-stress field."*

Women's Law **womenslaw.org** *"Because knowledge is power."*

ABOUT THE AUTHOR

Your
Photo
Here

ASHLEY WARNER is a writer and psychotherapist in private practice in New York City. When she's not in the office you might find her in the pottery studio covered with mud, salsa dancing, or crushing her husband at Scrabble. Syzygy.

Visit me:
ashleywarner.com
Goodreads: goodreads.com/ashleywarner
Twitter: @ashleywarnernyc
Facebook: @ashleywarnerauthor

Made in the USA
Columbia, SC
10 December 2024